SIMPLY ESSENTIAL
LANDLORD'S KIT

SIMPLY ESSENTIAL LANDLORD'S KIT

Timothy Madden

Self-Counsel Press
(a division of)
International Self-Counsel Press
USA   Canada

Self-Counsel Press acknowledges the financial support of the Government of Canada through the Book Publishing Industry Development Program for our publishing activities.

Printed in Canada.

First edition: 2002; Reprinted: 2003, 2004

National Library of Canada Cataloguing in Publication Data

Madden, Timothy.
     Simply essential landlord's kit

     ISBN 1-55180-384-4

     1. Landlord and tenant.   2. Rental housing—Management—Forms.   I. Title.
HD1394.M28 2002   333.33'8   C2002-910359-2

Self-Counsel Press
(*a division of*)
International Self-Counsel Press Ltd.

1481 Charlotte Road	1704 N. State Street
North Vancouver, BC V7J 1H1	Bellingham, WA 98225
Canada	USA

CONTENTS

NOTICE TO READERS

Laws are constantly changing. Every effort is made to keep this publication as current as possible. However, the author, the publisher, and the vendor make no representation or warranties regarding the outcome or the use to which the information in this book is put. This book is not a substitute for professional advice and cannot by its very nature address special problems or problems unique to individuals or the communities where they live. It is always best to consult licensed lawyers, accountants, and other professionals in your own community. We recommend that you consult your local rent control agency (or the equivalent) regarding the use of the *Simply Essential Landlord's Kit* in your area.

The rental agreement forms (forms A2.1, A2.2, A2.3, and A2.4) are examples of rental agreements. Please consult your local rent control agency, rental tribunal (or the equivalent) for regulations that may be specific to your area, then modify the form on disk to suit your needs.

GETTING STARTED

Congratulations on your purchase of the *Simply Essential Landlord's Kit*. You have just taken the first step toward managing your property more effectively.

While no program can guarantee success, this kit should help make things go a little more smoothly for you, reducing the number of headaches often associated with property management. You probably will not need to use all of the forms and checklists in the *Simply Essential Landlord's Kit*, since every rental situation is a little different, but feel free to experiment.

Using This Book

Here are some tips to help you use the *Simply Essential Landlord's Kit* efficiently, as well as some tips to help ensure your success:

- Some of the forms in this kit require you (or your representative) to circle or check the appropriate word or phrase (e.g., **month\week** or ✔ Principle tenant, etc.). Read each form carefully, circle or check all items that apply to your situation, and ensure that each form has been properly completed.

- Signatures are always very important. Documents should never be left unsigned.

- When making changes to any A-Series form, all parties signing the form should also initial the changes.

- If you must make changes to any form, use white-out to make changes before you make multiple copies of the form; or better yet, make changes to the CD-ROM copy of the form, then print out the updated version. When using the CD-ROM copies of the forms, you may wish to print out forms double sided (e.g., Rental Application/ Rental Agreement) to save on paper. Or you can photocopy the forms double sided.

- It is important to make copies of some completed forms (particularly of the A Series: Forms for Management and Tenants), such as Damage Inspection, Termination of Tenancy, Rental Agreement, and Pet Application. Keep the original for your records and give your tenant(s) the copy. When in doubt, copy it.

- Never assume that common sense will prevail, as common sense for you may not be common sense for somebody else. People often require things to be spelled out. Being direct may help to eliminate the guesswork involved in managing your property.

- It is a good idea to join a credit-reporting agency in your area. The small price you pay for receiving credit information about a prospective tenant may save you problems in the future.

- Always call the references provided by a prospective tenant as soon as possible after the application is received. Many people list only the persons, employers, and credit references whom they are sure will provide outstanding referrals; however, you may be surprised if you call. Your gut feeling combined with the information gathered from these references and the Rental Application form are all that you have to go on.

Forms and Descriptions

Below is a list of the forms provided in the *Simply Essential Landlord's Kit*, along with a brief description of each.

A Series: Forms for Management and Tenants

1. Prospective Tenants

A1.1   **Rental Application:** Basic application, plenty of references. Concentrates mostly on present/past addresses. For landlords seeking long-term tenants.

A1.2   **Application for Tenancy:** Basic application.

A1.3   **Rental Application:** Excellent for landlords renting houses or large apartments to multiple tenants.

A1.4   **Rental Application:** Basic application, packed with information.

2. Approved Tenants

A2.1   **Rental Agreement:** Standard rental agreement.

A2.2   **Rental Agreement:** An in-depth rental agreement.

A2.3   **Rental Agreement:** For the more particular.

A2.4   **Rental Application and Agreement:** Both in one form. Brief, but to the point.

A2.5   **Notice of Rent Increase:** Time for a rent increase? This form spells it out to your tenants.

A2.6   **Last Month's Rent Payment Schedule:** When approved applicants cannot pay the last month's rent (LMR) in full before moving in, use this form to set up a schedule for payment(s), which can become part of the Rental/Tenancy Agreement.

3. Pets

A3.1   **Pet Application:** Tenants and prospective tenants must complete this form, which must be approved by you before they are allowed to bring pets into the premises.

4. Ending a Tenancy

A4.1 **Request to Terminate Tenancy:** When a tenant wishes to terminate a tenancy, he or she completes this form so that you have a written record of the request. If you rent the unit to somebody else and the tenant does not move, you have a written record you can use in court. You will thank yourself over and over if this situation ever happens and you used this form to get the notice in writing.

A4.2 **Notice of Termination of Tenancy:** If, for any reason, you decide that you no longer wish to rent to a particular tenant, this form will give that tenant notice of your desire. (**Note:** Most Landlord and Tenant Acts (or their equivalents) do not allow a landlord to terminate a tenancy without a valid reason. Check your local act for details before completing this form.)

A4.3 **Agreement to Terminate a Tenancy:** Use this form when — for whatever reason — you and your tenant agree to terminate the tenancy. It provides you with a record of the agreement, should you ever need to go to court to enforce it.

5. Problems, Requests, and Damages

A5.1 **Tenant Complaint:** When a tenant has a complaint, he or she may be too upset to explain the problem to you in a polite manner. Words may fail the tenant when he or she is talking to you. By providing this form, you give your tenant the opportunity to put words to paper (and even draw diagrams), allowing him or her the chance to properly explain the problem to you. In addition, you will have a record of the complaint in case you forget details or in the event of repeated problems.

A5.2 **Tenant Request/Complaint:** This form is similar to form A5.1, but includes tenant requests (for tenants who wish to paint, wallpaper, etc.) and space for you to document (for future reference) what was done in response to the request or complaint.

A5.3 **Permission to Use:** You may wish to have a say in what items (appliances, barbecues, heaters, etc.) your tenants may use, particularly if you are paying the utilities. This form lets you set the terms for use of, monitor the use of, or rescind permission to use these and other items.

A5.4 **Rent in Arrears:** If a tenant does not pay rent or the rent check bounces, give him or her this completed form and keep a copy for your records.

A5.5 **Damage Inspection:** Completing this form when each tenant moves into and out of each unit will provide a reference for you of what (if anything) was damaged by the tenant during his or her tenancy. It may also aid you in recognizing a problem you might otherwise not have noticed, and gives you — at a glance — a record of the condition of each unit. Use this form in conjunction with form A5.6.

A5.6 **Supplemental Damage Inspection (kitchen and bathroom):** Use this form in conjunction with form A5.5. This form is more detailed regarding kitchens and bathrooms.

A5.7 **Damage Report:** This form is an alternative to A5.5 and A5.6. Use one page for each room or area.

6.   Ownership/Management Changes

A6.1 **Notice of New Owner/Manager:** If you are buying or selling a property, you can use this form to give the tenants information about who now owns the property, to whom they should pay the rent, whom they should call, etc.

A6.2 **Notice of New Ownership:** If you are buying or selling a property, this form will give the tenants information about the new property owner and whom to contact about tenancy matters.

A6.3 **Notice of Appointment of Manager:** If there is a management change for any reason (whether you wish to have less to do with day-to-day operations or choose to replace the existing manager), this form will explain the changes to your tenants so that they know whom to contact about tenancy matters.

A6.4 **Acknowledgment of Tenancy:** If you are considering purchasing a new property, have the existing owner complete this form. It may save you problems . . . or even lawsuits.

7. General

A7.1 **Fire Emergency Procedures (occupants):** Use this form to let your tenants know what to do in case the fire alarm system sounds.

A7.2 Laundry Room Hours/Rules: Laundry room hours and rules are a must for buildings with laundry facilities. Post this form in your laundry room.

A7.3 Laundry Schedule: Place this completed schedule in the laundry area and give each tenant a copy. Each tenant is guaranteed a specific time and day to do his/her laundry. Free times will give any tenant the opportunity to do laundry other than at his or her scheduled times. You will thank yourself for using this schedule, and your tenants will too.

B Series: Forms for Management Only

1. Money

B1.1 Monthly Cash Flow Summary: Plot your monthly expenses to keep track of where your money is made and where your money is spent. Compare this month's totals to the same month last year to see if you are making or spending more or less money.

B1.2 Annual Cash Flow Summary: Plot your yearly expenses to keep track of where your money is made and where your money is spent. Compare this year's totals to last year's totals to see if you are making or spending more or less money. This is a great form to use for income-tax purposes.

B1.3 Utility Log: Plot your monthly utility bills to keep track of how much money each building or unit is costing you each month and year as well as your average monthly cost. This form may be used in determining how much to charge for monthly rent.

B1.4 Laundry Revenue: Keep track of your laundry revenues and other laundry-related data.

2. Names/Phone Numbers

B2.1 Master Tenant List: This form provides you with a brief synopsis of five rental units, complete with phone numbers. A handy reference to have in the event of an emergency or a mass telephoning agenda.

B2.2 Tenant List: This form provides you with a brief synopsis of seven rental units, complete with phone numbers and rent information. A handy reference to have in the event of an emergency or a mass telephoning agenda.

B2.3 **Tenant Information:** This form provides you with a brief synopsis of each rental unit, complete with phone numbers, rent information, laundry times, pets, automobile information, etc.

B2.4 **Tenant List:** This form is your basic tenant list: ten names, addresses, and telephone numbers.

B2.5 **Service-Provider List:** Use this form to list the service providers you use or may need to call if there is a problem (e.g., plumber, appliance repair, painter, etc.).

3. Maintenance

B3.1 **Paint Information:** A must for any property owner. If you ever need to repaint or touch up a painted surface, you have complete records of the kind and color of paint you used the first time, even if you misplaced any leftover paint cans. No more guessing wrong and repainting an entire room or unit when only a touch-up is required.

B3.2 **Maintenance Log:** Keep track of maintenance performed in each unit as well as who performed the work and how much it cost. Complete this maintenance log yourself or have your maintenance personnel complete it as work is done. A handy reference for routine maintenance schedules or to pinpoint problem maintenance issues.

B3.3 **Maintenance Log:** Keep track of dates, work done, and time spent by you or your maintenance staff in the day-to-day maintenance of your property. A handy reference for routine maintenance schedules or to pinpoint problem maintenance issues.

B3.4 **Spring Checklist:** A helpful checklist to remind you to do certain tasks at the right time of the year.

B3.5 **Summer Checklist:** A helpful checklist to remind you to do certain tasks at the right time of the year.

B3.6 **Fall Checklist:** A helpful checklist to remind you to do certain tasks at the right time of the year.

B3.7 **Winter Checklist:** A helpful checklist to remind you to do certain tasks at the right time of the year.

B3.8 **Job Estimate/Quote:** Sooner or later, your building(s) will need repair. Most reputable repair contractors will provide you with a signed estimate or quote. Many will have their own forms, but some may not. If the latter is the case, have the contractor fill out this form. Make sure that clean-up is included in any quote or you may get stuck cleaning up the mess left by repair personnel.

4. Inventory

B4.1 **Equipment Inventory:** This information may prove to be invaluable in the event of theft, fire loss, or other loss. You may possibly obtain a more comprehensive inventory list from your insurance agent, but we recommend that you give your insurance agent a copy of whichever list you use and update it whenever you purchase additional equipment.

B4.2 **Utilities and Appliance Inventory:** Use this form to record information about utilities (furnace, boiler, water heater, etc.) and major appliances (refrigerators, stoves, dishwashers, disposers, etc.) so that you have a record of when they were bought as well as their prices, model, and serial numbers.

5. Fire Safety

B5.1 **Fire Safety Checklist:** This is one version of the responsibilities of the owner (or the agent for the owner) regarding fire safety. You must check with your local Fire Department to obtain a complete list of responsibilities for owners in your community and to obtain a copy of your local Fire Code.

B5.2 **Fire Inspection Checklist:** Use this checklist in conjunction with form B5.1 to record your safety checks.

B5.3 **Fire Emergency Procedures (Management):** This form tells you what to do in case the fire alarm system sounds. Read it often and practice regularly.

Creating a Rental Advertisement

Creating a rental advertisement is a very important undertaking. Poorly worded ads will get little response, making the job of renting a unit all the more difficult. Your advertisement needs to answer as many questions as possible, without being too long and boring, to let you zero in on people who are looking for what you are offering. The more people who see your ad, the better your chances of renting the unit.

Some of the most crucial details you must include in your ad are price, type of unit for rent, location, available facilities or services, what is/is not included in the rent, your preferences, and your telephone number. Unless your advertising budget is unlimited, you will have to convey all this information with as few words as possible.

When creating your ad, keep the following in mind:

- **Price:** Some landlords do not list the price in the advertisement at all, though it is strongly advised to do so. If you do not include price, prospective tenants will likely go on to read the rest of the "for rent" ads, ignoring yours.

- **Type of unit:** Most prospective tenants know whether they are looking for a one- or two-bedroom apartment or a three-bedroom house. If you tell them in your ad what size of accommodation you have available, you'll avoid calls from people looking for a three-bedroom house when you are trying to rent a one-bedroom apartment.

- **Location:** Stating in your ad where the unit you wish to rent is located will also help you avoid unnecessary telephone calls. You may list the exact address, basic area (e.g., downtown area), or something in between.

- **Facilities/services:** Fridge and stove, four-piece bath, coin-op laundry, parking, view of the lake, fenced yard, on-site superintendent are examples of facilities/services you could list.

- **Included/not included:** If you pay for the heat and hot water, but the tenant is responsible for paying the electricity, say so in your ad. If the tenant pays for heating, list the type of heating system (e.g., electric, forced air, gas, etc.). List in your ad either what is included or what is not included in the rent, or both.

- **Preferences:** You may prefer to rent to nonsmoking tenants or have a no-pets policy. You may prefer to rent to couples only, families only, or one tenant only. If you have specific preferences, say so in your ad.

- **Telephone number:** The telephone number is by far the most important part of your ad. If prospective tenants cannot get in touch with you, you may never rent the unit. List all telephone numbers at which you can be reached while your ad is running. If you wish to receive calls only at specific times (e.g., evenings or weekends), say so. Many prospective tenants do not leave messages on answering machines, so try to tell them how and when to get hold of you. Do whatever it takes to be there to answer all calls.

Fitting all this information into your advertisement is an art. Check your local publications for examples of ads in your area. Don't be afraid to be creative with your advertisement: the more eyes that are attracted to your advertisement, the better your chance of success. Try borders, headlines, or anything else that may attract more attention to your ad. Try to avoid listing the negative aspects of the unit, but never be deceitful. Always be honest when advertising and when answering questions about the unit.

PART 1:
A SERIES: FORMS
FOR MANAGEMENT
AND TENANTS

A1.1 — RENTAL APPLICATION

(Each applicant must complete a separate Rental Application)

The undersigned hereby makes application to rent the_____apartment at

_____at a monthly rent of $_____plus/including_____.

_____Principle tenant　　　_____Additional tenant (room-mate)　　Date required_____

Name_____ SIN#/SSN#_____

Address_____ Phone #_____

Name of present landlord_____ Phone #_____

Reason you are moving_____

How long have you lived at present address? _____years _____months

If less than one year, please provide the following:

Previous address_____ How long?_____

Name of previous landlord_____ Phone #_____

Reason for leaving_____

May I/we call your present/previous landlord? _____yes _____no

If no, why?_____

Have you ever been evicted? _____yes _____no

If yes, why?_____

Will others be occupying the premises? _____yes _____no

Name(s)_____

Are you:　_____**employed**　_____full-time　_____part-time

　　　　　　Where?_____How long?_____

　　　　_____**on assistance**　Type_____

　　　　_____**a student**　Where?_____

　　　　_____**other**　Explain_____

Supervisor, case worker, etc._____Phone #_____Ext._____

May I/we call your supervisor, case worker , etc.? _____yes _____no

If no, why?_____

Please provide two personal references (non-family)

Name_____Occupation_____Phone #_____

Name_____Occupation_____Phone #_____

The information collected in this application will be kept strictly confidential, and will be used only to evaluate your suitability as a tenant. If your application is approved, a security deposit equal to one month's rent will be required prior to acceptance and first month's rent will be required prior to occupancy. Thereafter, rent will be due on or before the_____day of every month.

The above information is, to the best of my knowledge, true and correct.

Signature_____ Date_____

A1.2 — APPLICATION FOR TENANCY

(Each applicant and co-applicant (room-mate) must apply separately.)

Applicant name:_____ Address:_____

How long:_____ Phone #:_____ Current rent: $_____ Monthly income: $_____

Reason(s) for moving:_____

Name(s) of everyone who will be living in the unit:_____

Landlord:_____ Phone #:_____

Employer:_____ Phone #:_____

Occupation (job title):_____ How long employed?:_____

Automobile: Year:_____ Make:_____ Model:_____ Color:_____

Driver's license #:_____ License plate #:_____

REFERENCES: (non-family)

Name:_____ Address:_____

Occupation:_____ Phone #:_____

Name:_____ Address:_____

Occupation:_____ Phone #:_____

This application is to be binding upon the applicant(s) for a period of seven days from the date completed, during which time this application shall be open for acceptance by, or on behalf of, the landlord. Deposit to be returned to the applicant(s) only if this application is **not** accepted by the landlord within the seven days. If approved, this application will form part of the tenancy agreement, and the deposit will be applied towards the payment of the security deposit. Any false or misleading statements are cause for immediate termination of tenancy.

_____   _____   _____
(applicant signature)   (print name)   (date)

(office use)

Monthly rent:_____ plus/including:_____ Deposit paid: $_____

_____Single applicant **OR** _____Primary applicant _____Co-applicant #1 _____Co-applicant #2

_____   _____   _____
(landlord or agent signature)   (print name)   (date)

Accepted/denied this_____day of_____, _____.

A1.3 — RENTAL APPLICATION

Date:_____

ABOUT THE PREMISES:

Address:_____ Unit #:_____ Type:_____

Rent: $_____ /(day, week, month, year) _____First only _____First & last _____Deposit: $_____

_____No parking _____Parking for_____vehicle(s) (outside, garage, car port, underground) Fee: $_____

The following utilities are included: _____Heat _____Electricity _____Gas _____Water _____Hot water

_____Cable t.v. _____Pay t.v. _____Telephone _____ _____ (use back if necessary)

The following appliances are included: _____Refrigerator _____Range _____Hot plate _____Toaster oven

_____Dishwasher _____Garbage disposal _____Microwave oven _____Freezer _____Washer _____Dryer

_____Air conditioner _____ _____ _____ _____ (use back if necessary)

The following furnishings are included:_____

_____(use back if necessary)

ABOUT THE APPLICANT(S):

	Applicant #1	Applicant #2	Applicant #3
Name			
Address			
How long?			
Phone #			
SIN#/SSN#			
Landlord			
Phone #			
Employer			
How long?			
Phone #			

By signing below, you declare that all information above is true and correct.

Signature			

A1.4 — RENTAL APPLICATION

Date:_____

Name of applicant_____ Age_____ Phone #_____

Names of others who will live at the premises_____

Number and type of pets who will live at the premises_____

Current address_____ How long?_____ Current rent $_____

Current landlord_____ Phone #_____ Ext._____

If less than 2 years at present address, list previous address information below.

Previous address_____ How long?_____ Previous rent $_____

Employer_____ How long?_____ Monthly salary $_____

Supervisor at work_____ Phone #_____ Ext._____

If employed less than 2 years with above employer, list previous employer information below.

Employer_____ How long?_____ From_____to_____

Supervisor at work_____ Phone #_____ Ext._____

Credit references   1. _____ Phone #_____

2. _____ Phone #_____

Personal references   1. _____ Phone #_____

2. _____ Phone #_____

Driver's license #_____ SIN #/SSN#_____

By signing below, you certify that the information supplied above is true and correct, and that you give permission to the Landlord or Agent for the Landlord to obtain a credit check and/or verify that the information supplied above is true. An application deposit of $_____ is required before this application will be considered for acceptance (to be applied to the security deposit if accepted, or refunded if rejected). Any false or misleading statements made in this application may be cause for immediate termination of the tenancy, if accepted, and/or forfeiture of any deposit(s) given in association with this application. If you are accepted for occupancy, but decline to accept the premises applied for, for any reason, then the application deposit will not be refunded. A security deposit of $_____(less application deposit) is required before occupancy (to be refunded only after premises have been vacated, providing it has been adequately cleaned and any damage has been repaired).

Signature of applicant_____

A2.1 — RENTAL AGREEMENT
(To be completed after acceptance and prior to occupancy)

_____ (**tenant**) and_____(**co-tenant**) herein rent

through _____ (**Agent for the owner**, or **Owner**) the premises at the address

commonly known as _____ at a monthly rent of $ _____,

plus/including (**circle**)_____, to be due and payable on or before

the first day of each and every month by the tenant to the owner or his/her agent. This Rental Agreement

begins on _____ (**D/M/Y**) (subject, if premises currently occupied, to present tenant

vacating) and will remain in effect until the tenancy is terminated.

Additional co-tenant(s) are as follows :_____

THIS AGREEMENT IS SUBJECT TO THE FOLLOWING CONDITIONS

The tenant and the co-tenant(s) (if applicable) agree(s):

1. not to keep any pets on the premises without **first** obtaining specific written permission (application to be filled out) from the owner or his/her agent.
2. to keep the premises as a private dwelling only.
3. to be responsible for obtaining insurance for personal items kept in or on the premises.
4. not to assign or sublet the premises or any part thereof or to make alterations without prior written consent from the owner or his/her agent, and agrees that all future co-tenants must apply, and be approved, **prior** to occupancy.
5. to keep the premises (including the grounds) clean, free from refuse, and in good repair, and to keep clean, and repair any damages, while residing in the premises as well as when vacating the premises.
6. to use the premises as they were designed to be used. If the premises are not designed specifically to allow the hook-up of a washer, dryer, dishwasher, air conditioner, etc., then the installation and use of these appliances is strictly forbidden (even the occasional use of the above-mentioned appliances is in specific violation of this agreement).
7. that waterbeds are **not** permitted in the premises.
8. to give **two (2) full month's written notice** before vacating the premises (moving out).
9. to allow the owner or his/her agent to place a for rent sign in or on the premises during the last month of occupancy, and to allow persons interested in viewing the premises to do so at any reasonable hour of any day of the week (or weekend).
10. that a maximum of ___ parking space(s) is allotted for the tenant (and co-tenant if applicable) and only if space is available **and** proof of vehicle ownership is provided.
11. that rent paid **after** the _____ day of the month **will** be subject to a $ _____ surcharge, and that N.S.F. (bounced) checks **will** be subject to a $ _____ fee.

Please read the above agreement carefully before signing in the area provided below.
By signing below, the Tenant, Co-tenant(s), and the Landlord/Agent agree to the above-listed terms.

_____   _____   _____
(tenant signature)   (print name)   (date)

_____   _____   _____
(co-tenant signature)   (print name)   (date)

_____   _____   _____
(witness signature)   (print name)   (date)

_____   _____   _____
(owner or agent signature)   (print name)   (date)

A2.2 — RENTAL AGREEMENT

_____(**Tenant(s)**) herein rent through _____

_____ (**Owner/Agent for the Owner**) the premises located at _____

Apt.# _____ for a **monthly/weekly** rent of $_____ **plus/including** _____ to be due

and payable on or before _____ of each and every **month/week** (subject, if premises

presently occupied, to present tenant(s) vacating). This agreement becomes effective on the _____ day of

_____, _____, and remains in effect until the end of the last day of the tenancy.

THE ABOVE LISTED TENANT(S) AGREE(S) TO (circle the number of each term that applies):

1. Pay for all damage(s) caused willfully, accidentally, or by neglect, whether caused by the tenant(s) or invited or uninvited visitor(s) of the tenant(s). Natural disasters and reasonable wear and tear excepted.
2. Not make any alterations to the premises (painting, wallpapering, window treatments, changing locks, etc.) without **first** obtaining permission from the Owner, or Agent for the Owner.
3. Not sublet or allow any person(s) or pet(s) to live at the premises without first obtaining permission from the Owner, or Agent for the Owner. The Owner reserves the right to increase the rent if additional person(s) or pet(s) are approved.
4. Pay a security deposit equal to one **month's/week's** rent prior to occupancy, or on a payment schedule agreed to by all parties (attach a copy of the payment schedule to this agreement), and refunded only after the premises have been vacated and the Owner or Agent for the Owner is satisfied that the premises are free of damage and have been adequately cleaned.
5. Allow the Owner and/or the Agent for the Owner to visually inspect the premises when collecting the rent.
6. Inform the Owner or Agent for the Owner of all damages and worn or non-working aspects of the premises (leaky taps, faulty appliances, clogged drains, etc.) as soon as possible, and to allow entry to service personnel when they are available.
7. Ensure that all smoke and carbon monoxide detectors located in the premises are fully functioning at all times and replace the batteries (if applicable), when needed, at no cost to the Owner or Agent for the Owner.
8. Keep the premises (including the grounds) clean, free from refuse, and in good repair.
9. Be responsible for obtaining insurance for the contents of the premises (personal possessions).
10. Respect the neighbors' right to peace and privacy at all times (day and night).
11. Never engage in any illegal activities in or on the premises (including operating a business).
12. Not install, or otherwise use, any of the following items without first obtaining specific written approval from the Owner or Agent for the Owner: Dishwasher, Washing machine, Dryer, Space heater or auto heaters, Barbecue, Air conditioner, Antenna, _____, _____, _____.
13. Not use water-filled furniture in or on the premises (waterbed(s), hot tub(s), etc.).
14. Give a **minimum** of_____advance notice before vacating the premises.
15. Park in only the assigned parking space(s) located _____, and ensure that all visitors park in the visitor's parking area (if provided) located _____. Tenant(s) and visitor(s) park at their own risk.
16. Pay a late fee of $_____ for rent that is not paid **in full** on or before _____ of each and every **month/week**, and pay a fee of $_____ for N.S.F. (bounced) cheques.
17. Follow the rules and schedule for doing laundry. All above-listed tenants may lose their laundry privileges if the rules and schedule are not followed. Laundry use is restricted to tenants only.

PLEASE READ THE ABOVE AGREEMENT CAREFULLY BEFORE SIGNING IN THE SPACE PROVIDED. BY SIGNING BELOW, YOU AGREE TO THE TERMS INDICATED ABOVE. SIGN AND DATE IN THE PRESENCE OF ALL PARTIES.

_____   _____   _____
(Tenant signature)   (Tenant signature)   (Tenant signature)

_____   _____   _____
(Owner or Agent signature)   (Witness signature)   (Date)

20

A2.3 — RENTAL AGREEMENT

This **Rental Agreement** between the **Landlord**_____ and the **Tenant**
_____, as **Witnessed** by _____, for the **Premises**
known as (Address)_____, located on the
Property owned by_____, shall commence on (Date)_____.

The rent ($_____) shall be paid to_____ on or before
the _____of each and every_____. Checks and money orders shall be made payable to_____
_____ **(no cash payments please)**. Rent paid **after** the due date may be
subject to a **late payment** charge of $_____, and **N.S.F. cheques** may be subject to a charge of
$_____. A deposit of $_____has been paid (or shall be paid according to the following
schedule:
_____),
and shall be (check one)   [   ] applied as the final rental payment.

[   ] returned after the **Tenant** vacates the **Premises** and returns the key, and
the **Landlord** is satisfied that the **Premises** have been adequately cleaned
and any irregularities have been corrected by, and at the expense of, the
Tenant.

This Tenancy Agreement may be terminated by the Landlord for any of the following reasons (providing local laws permit): Current rent is not paid; Frequent late payments; Damage to the Premises and/or the Property by the Tenant and/or the Tenant's guest(s); Illegal act(s) or business; Interfering with the safety of the Landlord and/or others; Disturbing others; Keeping a pet and/or room-mate without permission from the Landlord; Landlord requires the Premises for his/her own use; Demolition or major repairs or renovations; Any other reason deemed lawful according to local regulation.

This Tenancy Agreement may be terminated by the Tenant providing at least 60 days' notice (in writing) has been given.

Where the rent for the Premises includes Utilities (heat, electricity, water, etc.) then the Tenant shall use the Utilities responsibly. Heaters, air conditioners, and other "high drain" appliances are forbidden to be used unless an additional fee is paid. The Landlord reserves the right to restrict the temperature of the heating and/or cooling systems to the guideline temperature for the area, as directed by local laws.

All lightbulbs in the Premises shall be replaced by the Tenant at no cost to the Landlord. Snow removal and lawn maintenance are the responsibility of the (circle one) **Landlord/Tenant**. Storage areas, if provided, must be kept tidy, and are used at the Tenant's risk. Where laundry facilities are provided, the Tenant shall abide by the rules posted. Garbage must be properly secured in plastic bags (no boxes) and placed neatly in the garbage area. Pet owners must clean up after their pets, and place feces and litter in plastic bags, double bagged. Where parking space(s) are provided, park only in the space(s) assigned and inform your guests of the parking arrangements. The Tenant shall inform the Landlord, in a timely manner, of any damages, faulty appliances, dripping or leaky water pipes, or other maintenance issues pertaining to the Premises and/or the Property.

By signing below, the Landlord and Tenant agree to the terms of this Tenancy Agreement.

_____   _____   _____
Tenant signature and date   **Landlord** signature and date   **Witness** signature and date

21

A2.4 — RENTAL APPLICATION AND AGREEMENT

(Single occupancy only. No room-mates.)

APPLICATION

Date of Application:_____ Date unit required:_____

Address of unit being applied for:_____ Rent: $_____

Name:_____ Phone #:_____

Current address:_____ Current rent: $_____

How long?_____ Why moving?_____ Age (optional):_____

Current landlord:_____ May we contact current landlord?_____

Address:_____ Phone #:_____

Employer:_____ How long?_____ Monthly wage: $_____

Address:_____ Phone #:_____

Reference 1: Name:_____ Phone #:_____

Reference 2: Name:_____ Phone #:_____

AGREEMENT

If your application is approved, the following terms represent the rental agreement:

1. This unit shall remain a single occupancy rental unit. Guests may stay no longer than_____.
2. Tenant must keep the unit reasonably clean, and dispose of all garbage in the designated area(s).
3. Tenant is responsible for the conduct of his/her guests, whether invited or not.
4. No pets allowed without prior written approval from the Landlord.
5. No painting, wallpapering, or any other alterations without prior written approval from the Landlord.
6. The Landlord reserves the right to inspect the unit at any given time, providing 24 hours' notice (written or oral) has been given, or when collecting the rent.
7. No waterbeds are permitted to be used in the unit.
8. _____notice is required before moving.
9. A late fee of $_____ will be charged if rent is not paid in full on or before_____.
10. A fee of $_____ will be charged for all N.S.F. (bounced) checks returned from the bank.

By signing below, you certify that the information in the Application is true, and that you agree to the terms of the Agreement, and that you give permission to the landlord (or his/her agent) to verify that the above information is true. Any false or misleading statements are grounds for eviction and/or rejection of your Application.

_____   _____   _____
Applicant signature   Landlord (or Agent) signature   Witness signature

Please provide TWO pieces of ID:_____

_____

22

A2.5 — NOTICE OF RENT INCREASE

Tenant	**Landlord**
Name:_____	Name:_____
Address:_____	Address_____
_____	_____

Current rent is $_____ per _____. Last increased on_____, _____.

       On the following date,_____, _____, the rent for your unit will increase by $_____ (_____%). This percentage is in accordance with the guidelines set forth by the governing agency in this area. This will bring your total rental payment to $_____ per _____from the above date forward. The last_____ rent for your unit will also be raised by $____ and should be paid on or before the above date. The maximum rent allowable for your unit is $_____ per _____. The new rent includes the following:

Basic rent	$_____	
Parking	$_____	(_____ space(s), # _____)
Other	$_____	(_____)
Other	$_____	(_____)
Other	$_____	(_____)
Other	$_____	(_____)
Total	$_____	

       If any of the above information is incorrect, or if you have any questions, please contact me at _____ between the hours of _____ and _____, weekdays.

       Signed and dated this _____ day of _____, _____.

_____	_____	_____
print name	title	signature

23

A2.6 — LAST MONTH'S RENT PAYMENT SCHEDULE

Tenant:_____Address: _____

Rent: $_____per_____ Total L.M.R.: $_____ Date: _____

This schedule of payments for the last month's rent at the above address **is/is not** part of the Rental Agreement.

Date due	Payment due	Date paid	Payment made	Balance due
	$		$	$

By signing below, the Tenant agrees to make the **Payment due** on or before the **Date due**, and the Landlord/Agent for the Landlord agrees that this payment schedule is adequate for the completion of the last month's rent. If the Tenant fails to make the **Payment due** on or before the **Date due** then the Rental Agreement may be considered violated. Violation of the terms of a Rental Agreement may be just cause for the Landlord/Agent for the Landlord to terminate the tenancy.

_____   _____   _____
Tenant signature   Landlord/Agent signature   Witness signature

24

A3.1 — PET APPLICATION

I/We hereby request permission to bring _____ _____ into the building, as a house pet, to
                               (#)   (type of animal)

live at _____ .
                             (address)

1.   I understand that if my pet(s):
       - causes noise, odor(s), or damage;
       - and/or causes another tenant or the owner to have an allergic reaction, or phobia;
       - and/or harms or acts aggressively toward another tenant or the owner;
       - and/or could be dangerous to another tenant or the owner, even if it has not harmed anyone;
then my pet(s) is/are to be immediately removed from the premises, upon written notice from the owner or his
/her agent, never to return again (neither to live nor to visit). Failure to comply, upon service of said written
notice, may be cause for eviction proceedings to commence immediately.
2.   All vaccinations to my pet(s) shall be up to date and verification shall be made available to the owner or
his/her agent upon request.
3.   No animal, mine or my guests, shall be permitted to run at large in common areas of the premises and shall
be on a leash and under adult supervision while in common areas of the premises, and shall not be permitted to
be tied up outside or in common areas of the premises.
4.   I am responsible for cleaning up after my pets and my guests' pet(s), should they create a mess on or in the
premises (including my apartment). <u>All</u> pet droppings shall be placed in a bag, securely sealed, and placed in
the garbage. <u>Under no circumstance should cat litter, etc., be flushed down the toilet or sink.</u>
5.   I am responsible for removal of any odors, fleas, mites, and repair of any damage that may be a result of
my having a pet, including cleaning carpet(s), fumigation, and repairing floors.

**Please read this agreement carefully before signing in the area provided below. Once signed, this
agreement becomes part of the rental agreement.**

_____   _____   _____
(tenant signature)   (print name)   (date)

_____   _____   _____
(co-tenant signature)   (print name)   (date)

_____   _____   _____
(witness signature)   (print name)   (date)

_____   _____   _____
(owner or agent signature)   (print name)   (date)

+--+
| (Office use) |
| |
| [   ] approved |
| |
| [   ] denied (specify reason (s)) _____ |
| |
| _____ |
+--+

A4.1 — REQUEST TO TERMINATE TENANCY

(Please print)

Landlord:_____   Agent for landlord: _____

Tenant:_____   Address:_____

I, _____ hereby request that my tenancy at the above
                        (Tenant name)
address be terminated on the_____day of_____ ,_____ . I understand that I
must deliver up vacant possession and occupation of the above premises on or before that date, and that
the premises must be adequately cleaned, and that the key(s) will be returned to the landlord or his/her
agent, and that this agreement may be enforced by a writ of possession (eviction order), or other court
action, at my expense, if I fail to do so. **Sign in the presence of the landlord or agent.**

Signed and dated this_____ day of_____ ,_____.

_____   _____
            (Tenant signature)   (Landlord/Agent signature)

(Office use)

[   ] Request denied (Give reason(s))_____

_____

_____

[   ] Request granted.   Conditions:_____

_____

_____

_____   _____
        (Landlord or agent signature)   (Date)

A4.2 — NOTICE OF TERMINATION OF TENANCY

Landlord/Agent for Landlord:_____ Phone #:_____
Tenant(s):_____ Address: _____

I,_____ hereby give notice that the above-mentioned tenant(s) give up vacant
  (Landlord/Agent for the Landlord)
possession (move out) of the above-mentioned address on or before the _____ day of _____, _____.

Reason(s): _____

_____

_____

_____

_____

_____

If the following conditions are adhered to indefinitely, this notice of termination shall become null and void:

_____

_____

_____

_____

_____

_____

_____

_____

_____

Signed and dated this_____ day of_____,_____.   _____
                                                                (Signature of Landlord/Agent for the Landlord)

27

A4.3 — AGREEMENT TO TERMINATE A TENANCY

Landlord/Agent for the Landlord:_____

Tenant(s):_____

Address:_____

    The above-listed parties hereby agree to terminate the tenancy with respect to the above listed premises on the _____ day of _____, _____.

    I/We, the tenant(s), upon signing below, agree to return the key(s) prior to vacating, and to clean and make good any repairs to the premises, and deliver up vacant possession of the premises on or before the above mentioned date and that this agreement may be enforced by legal action deemed necessary by the Landlord or the Agent for the Landlord at **my/our** expense, should **I/we** fail to comply with the terms of this agreement as well as the rental agreement, which was established at the beginning of the tenancy.

    The **Landlord/Agent for the Landlord**, upon signing below, agrees that the tenancy shall end on or before the above-mentioned date, providing the tenant(s) meet the obligations mentioned above.

Notes: _____

_____

_____

_____

_____

_____

_____

_____	_____
Tenant signature	date
_____	_____
Tenant signature	date
_____	_____
Witness signature	date
_____	_____
Landlord/Agent signature	date

28

A5.1 — TENANT COMPLAINT

Date: _____

Tenant name:_____Phone #: _____

Address:_____

Nature of complaint (check all that apply):   [   ]Noise   [   ] Damage   [   ] Parking

[   ] Odor   [   ] Pet(s)   [   ] Garbage   [   ] Rent   [   ] Laundry   [   ]Illegal activity

[   ] Unregistered occupants   [   ] Safety   [   ] Other _____

Describe, in detail, the nature of the complaint (include names, times, dates, details if possible.)

_____

_____

_____

_____

_____

_____

_____

_____

_____

_____

_____

_____

_____

_____

_____

_____

_____

_____

_____

_____

_____

_____
Signature

29

A5.2 — TENANT REQUEST/COMPLAINT

Name(s) of person(s) making the request/complaint _____

Address(es):_____Date:_____

In regards to: [   ] as above.

OR   [   ] Name(s):_____

                    Address(es):_____

Describe in detail, giving as much information about the request/complaint as possible, including times, dates, names, and actions taken where applicable. Use the back of this form and/or additional sheet(s) of paper if necessary. **Sign your name(s) at the end.**

Signature(s)

----- **Office use** -----

Action taken:

(Use additional sheet(s) of paper if necessary and attach copies of all relevant documents to this request/complaint)

Name:_____ Signature:_____ Date: _____

A5.3 — PERMISSION TO USE

Date:_____

This application, if approved, shall allow the Tenant _____

to use the items listed below with respect to the Premises located at_____

_____. If the Landlord pays the utilities for the above Premises, the Tenant agrees **not**

to use the item(s) listed below excessively (if applicable). The Landlord reserves the right to assign

guidelines, monitor the use, or rescind permission, with respect to the use of said items, at any time,

without explanation.

The proposed items are: _____

_____

_____

_____

_____

_____

_____

_____

The Landlord's conditions for the Tenant's use of the above items are: _____

_____

_____

_____

_____

_____

_____

[   ] Approved on (date)_____

[   ] Denied (specify reason(s))_____

_____

_____   _____
Tenant signature and date   **Landlord** or **Agent** signature and date

31

A5.4 — RENT IN ARREARS

TO: _____   FROM: _____

_____   _____

_____   _____

_____   _____

      Our records show that your rent is in arrears in the amount of $_____. A (circle one) **late Payment/N.S.F.** charge of $_____ shall be added to the above amount, for a combined total of $_____. Please pay this amount immediately by (circle all that apply) **cash/check/money order/certified check**. Payment of the above combined total not received, in full, on or before _____ (circle one) **shall/may** be cause for immediate eviction, unless alternate arrangements are agreed to. In the future, your rental payments (circle one) **shall/may** be required to be paid by (circle all that apply) **cash/check/money order/certified check**, and due on or before _____. Make checks or money orders payable to_____ _____ and deliver to_____at (address) _____, or call _____, between the hours of _____and _____.

      Non-payment of rent and/or frequent late rent and/or N.S.F. checks (circle one) **are/may be** cause for eviction, now and in the future.

      Signed and dated this _____ day of _____, _____.

_____
Landlord/Agent signature

A5.5 — DAMAGE INSPECTION

Tenant:_____ Address:_____ Date:_____

Inspection done by:_____ ___ Move in ___ Move out

(Leave space blank if item not damaged)

ROOMS INSPECTED					
Walls					
Ceiling					
Floor					
Trim					
Door(s)					
Window(s)					
Screen(s)					
Curtain(s)					
Blind(s)					
Shade(s)					
Heating					
Thermostat(s)					
Light(s)					
Switch(es)					
Receptacle(s)					
Phone					
Cable					

(Use back of page if more space is required.)

_____   _____   _____
Inspector signature   Tenant signature   Witness signature

A5.6 — SUPPLEMENTAL DAMAGE INSPECTION
(KITCHEN AND BATHROOM)

Tenant:_____   Address:_____   Date:_____

Inspection done by:_____   ___ Move in   ___ Move out

(Leave space blank if item not damaged)

	KITCHEN	BATHROOM #1	BATHROOM #2
Sink(s)			
Faucet(s)			
Clogs/Leaks			
Tub/Shower	N/A		
Toilet	N/A		
Counter top			
Cabinets			
Drawers			
Doors			
Vent. fan			
Silicone			

KITCHEN APPLIANCES

	Refrigerator	Range	Dishwasher		
Does it work?					
Door(s)					
Drawer(s)					
Shelves					
Light(s)					
Exterior					

_____   _____   _____
(Inspector signature)   (Tenant signature)   (Witness signature)

A5.7 — DAMAGE REPORT

(Use a separate sheet for each room or area inspected)

Tenant:_____ Address:_____ Date:_____

Inspection done by:_____ ___ Move in ___ Move out

Room/Area Inspected:_____

Walls/ceiling:

Floor:

Trim (window, door, baseboard, etc.):

Windows and doors (glass, screens, curtains, hardware, etc.):

Utilities (HVAC, electrical, cable, telephone, etc.):

Waterworks (sink, tub/shower, toilet, etc.):

Appliances:

Cabinetry (cabinets, counter top, shelving, etc.):

Other:

_____   _____   _____
Inspector signature   Tenant signature   Witness signature

A6.1 — NOTICE OF NEW OWNER/MANAGER

This notice is to inform you that a change of ownership has taken place for the premises located at
_____ effective_____.
(Date)

The new owner is _____

Address_____ Phone # _____

The new manager is _____

Address_____ Phone # _____

Beginning the above date all future correspondence regarding your tenancy should be directed to the **owner/manager** at the above address(es) and phone number(s). All future rents shall be paid to the **owner/manager** on or before the _____ day of each and every month, and payable by cash, money order, or check. All checks and money orders shall be made payable to _____. All N.S.F. checks may be subject to a $_____ charge in addition to the rent due. Rents paid after the _____ day of the month may be subject to a $_____ charge in addition to the rent due.

Our records show that your rent is currently set at $_____ per month. This includes_____
_____.

Please contact _____ immediately if these records are incorrect.

NOTE: _____
_____
_____
_____

Sincerely,

_____

_____

A6.2 — NOTICE OF NEW OWNERSHIP

This letter is to inform you that the premises located at_____

_____have recently come under new management as of

_____. The new owner of the premises is_____.

Please direct all future correspondence to:_____between

_____**AM/PM** and _____ **AM/PM daily/weekdays/weekends/**_____.

Our records show your rent as being $_____per **month/week, plus/including** _____

_____. If this is not correct, please phone the above number, or contact

_____ at _____.

NOTE: _____

_____

_____

_____

_____

_____

Sincerely,

_____

_____

A6.3 — <u>NOTICE OF APPOINTMENT OF MANAGER</u>

To: _____

_____

_____

This notice is to inform you that _____

will begin as manager of the premises located at_____

begining _____. The manager can be reached by telephone at_____

or in person at:_____**daily/weekdays/weekends**

between the hours_____**AM/PM** and_____ **AM/PM.** Please direct all future correspondence

regarding your tenancy to the manager beginning the above date. Please also pay your future rental

payments to the manager.

NOTE: _____

_____

_____

_____

_____

_____

Sincerely,

_____

_____

38

A6.4 — ACKNOWLEDGMENT OF TENANCY

Address _____

I,_____, hereby acknowledge that I am a tenant at the above

address and that other persons living at and/or using this address are as follows: _____

_____

I have been a tenant at this address since _____.

My rent is $_____ per **month/week**, payable on the _____ day of each **month/week**.

My rent is: [   ] paid in full until _____.

            [   ] in arrears in the amount of $_____.

My rent: [   ] was last increased on _____.

         [   ] has not increased since my tenancy began.

The last month's rent of $_____ has: [   ] been paid in full in the amount of $_____.

                  [   ] an outstanding balance of $_____.

                  [   ] not been paid.

There: [   ] is not a lease in effect for my tenancy at this address.

      [   ] is a lease in effect for my tenancy at this address which expires on _____.

I: [   ] have not given notice to vacate the premises.

    [   ] have not been served with a notice to vacate the premises.

    [   ] will be vacating the premises on _____.

In addition to the rent, I am responsible for the payment of :   [   ] Electricity,   [   ] Gas,

[   ] Taxes, [   ] Heat, [   ] Water,   [   ] Telephone,   [   ] Cable, [   ] Parking $_____,

[   ] Other _____.

The following items are furnished by the landlord: [   ] Refrigerator,   [   ] Stove,   [   ] Dryer,

[   ]Washer,   [   ] Dishwasher,   [   ] Other _____

      I hereby agree not to maintain any action, legal or otherwise, against any new owner of these premises, which may have occurred under the present ownership, or past ownership(s), of the premises. I also agree that my tenancy at this address may be subject to the completion of a Rental Application, Rental Agreement, or any other document(s) that any new owner may require to be completed (tenancy will **not** be subject to approval once the required documents have been properly completed).

Signed and dated this _____ day of _____, _____.

_____   _____   _____
tenant signature   witness signature   witness name (print)

A7.1 — FIRE EMERGENCY PROCEDURES (Occupants)
(A more complete listing may be obtained from your local Fire Department.)

IF YOU DISCOVER A FIRE:

1. Remain calm.
2. Leave the fire area, closing all doors behind you.
3. Activate the building fire alarm system using the closest fire alarm pull station (usually located at all exits).
4. Fight the fire only if you are confident that it may be controlled with the fire fighting equipment available.
5. Evacuate using the exit staircase and proceed to the main lobby to inform the superintendent of the fire location.
6. Ensure that the Fire Department has been called. If nobody can confirm that the Fire Department has been called, call them yourself from a phone **not** located in the building. Call **911** or _____.

IF YOU HEAR THE BUILDING FIRE ALARM:

1. Remain calm.
2. Leave the building using the closest exit staircase.
3. Before opening your suite door, test the door and the knob for heat.
4. If the door is hot, remain in you'r suite, or evacuate through the fire exit located in your suite (if provided).
5. If the door is cool to the touch, open it slightly and check the corridor for smoke. If the corridor is filled with smoke, remain in your suite or evacuate through the fire exit located in your suite (if provided). If the corridor is clear, proceed to the closest exit staircase. If all of the staircases are impassable, return to your suite and evacuate through the fire exit located in your suite (if provided).
6. **NEVER** use an elevator to escape a fire.
7. If you must remain in your suite, place damp towels or tape around the door frame to prevent smoke from entering your suite.
8. If the smoke enters your suite, proceed to the balcony or window, closing (but not locking) the door(s) behind you. Signal the Fire Department of your location using a towel or sheet.

ALWAYS:
1. Remain calm.
2. Evacuate the building immediately upon hearing the fire alarm as per above instructions.
3. Close doors and windows behind you as you exit the building, but **never** lock them.
4. Plan ahead. Practice your escape route(s) regularly so that you will be prepared to act when necessary.
5. Stay near the floor if you must evacuate through a smoke-filled corridor. Smoke rises, so the clearest air will be at floor level. Breath sparingly and move as quickly as possible toward the nearest exit.

NEVER:
1. Ignore a fire alarm when it sounds. **Always** assume that this is the real thing, and evacuate immediately.
2. Go back into a burning building to save pets or personal possessions—no matter how valuable they are to you.
3. Run or walk upright in a smoke-filled corridor.
4. Use an elevator to escape a fire.

40

A7.2 — LAUNDRY ROOM HOURS/RULES

_____ **TO** _____
(open)   (closed)

Wash $ _____ (approximately _____ minutes).

NO REFUNDS

Dry $ _____ (approximately _____ minutes).

Please empty lint tray after <u>each</u> dryer load.

Please don't leave clothes in machines when finished.

Please inform management of any damaged/broken machines.

Please do not sit on machines.

Please keep laundry area clean.

_____

_____

_____

_____

_____

_____

_____

Management not responsible for lost, stolen, or damaged items.

A7.3 — LAUNDRY SCHEDULE

(**FREE** times indicate that any Tenant may use the facilities on a first-come, first-served basis.)

TIME	MONDAY	TUESDAY	WEDNESDAY	THURSDAY	FRIDAY	SATURDAY	SUNDAY
	apt. #1	apt. #2	apt. #3	apt. #4	apt. #5	FREE	FREE

NOTE:_____

_____

_____

PART 2:
B SERIES: FORMS
FOR MANAGEMENT
ONLY

B1.1 — MONTHLY CASH-FLOW SUMMARY

Month:_____ Year:_____

INCOME (A)			EXPENSES (B)		
Source	Amount $	Last year $	Source	Amount $	Last year $
TOTAL A			TOTAL B		

Net income (**TOTAL A – TOTAL B**): $_____

NOTES:_____

_____

_____

_____

_____

B1.2 — ANNUAL CASH-FLOW SUMMARY

Months:_____to_____   Year:_____

INCOME (A)			EXPENSES (B)		
Month	Amount $	Last year $	Month	Amount $	Last year $
January			January		
February			February		
March			March		
April			April		
May			May		
June			June		
July			July		
August			August		
September			September		
October			October		
November			November		
December			December		
TOTAL A			**TOTAL B**		

Net income (**TOTAL A –TOTAL B**): $_____

NOTES:_____

_____

_____

_____

_____

_____

B1.3 — UTILITY LOG

Address: _____ Year: _____

Electricity account # _____

Gas company account # _____

Water account # _____

Other (_____) account # _____

Other (_____) account # _____

Month	Electricity	Gas	Water		
January	$	$	$	$	$
February					
March					
April					
May					
June					
July					
August					
September					
October					
November					
December					
TOTAL					
AVERAGE					

NOTES: _____

_____

_____

_____

_____

_____

B1.4 — LAUNDRY REVENUE

A = Washer: $_____per cycle

B = Dryer: $_____per cycle

C	D	E	F	G	H	J	K	L
Date	Washer $	Dryer $	Total $ D+E	# Washer loads D/__(A)	# Dryer loads E/__(B)	# of days since last emptied.	$ / Day (Avg.) F / J	# of Tenants
(e.g.)	25.00	18.00	43.00	20	24	27	1.59	6
(e.g.)	23,75	16.50	40.25	19	22	19	2.12	6
(e.g.)	31.25	18.75	50.00	25	25	31	1.61	5

NOTES:_____

_____

_____

B2.1 — MASTER TENANT LIST

Name:_____ Address:_____Phone #:_____

Employer:_____Phone #:_____

In emergency, contact:_____Phone #:_____

Total # of residents in the unit:_____ Name(s): _____

———

Name:_____ Address:_____Phone #:_____

Employer:_____Phone #:_____

In emergency, contact:_____Phone #:_____

Total # of residents in the unit:_____ Name(s): _____

———

Name:_____ Address:_____Phone #:_____

Employer:_____Phone #:_____

In emergency, contact:_____Phone #:_____

Total # of residents in the unit:_____ Name(s): _____

———

Name:_____ Address:_____Phone #:___._____

Employer:_____Phone #:_____

In emergency, contact:_____Phone #:_____

Total # of residents in the unit:_____ Name(s): _____

———

Name:_____ Address:_____Phone #:_____

Employer:_____Phone #:_____

In emergency, contact:_____Phone #:_____

Total # of residents in the unit:_____ Name(s): _____

B2.2 — TENANT LIST

_____ _____ _____
(Unit #)   (Address)   (Phone #)
_____ $_____
(Name(s))   (Rent)

_____ _____ _____
(Emergency contact person)   (Relationship)   (Phone #)

_____ _____ _____
(Unit #)   (Address)   (Phone #)
_____ $_____
(Name(s))   (Rent)

_____ _____ _____
(Emergency contact person)   (Relationship)   (Phone #)

_____ _____ _____
(Unit #)   (Address)   (Phone #)
_____ $_____
(Name(s))   (Rent)

_____ _____ _____
(Emergency contact person)   (Relationship)   (Phone #)

_____ _____ _____
(Unit #)   (Address)   (Phone #)
_____ $_____
(Name(s))   (Rent)

_____ _____ _____
(Emergency contact person)   (Relationship)   (Phone #)

_____ _____ _____
(Unit #)   (Address)   (Phone #)
_____ $_____
(Name(s))   (Rent)

_____ _____ _____
(Emergency contact person)   (Relationship)   (Phone #)

_____ _____ _____
(Unit #)   (Address)   (Phone #)
_____ $_____
(Name(s))   (Rent)

_____ _____ _____
(Emergency contact person)   (Relationship)   (Phone #)

_____ _____ _____
(Unit #)   (Address)   (Phone #)
_____ $_____
(Name(s))   (Rent)

_____ _____ _____
(Emergency contact person)   (Relationship)   (Phone #)

B2.3 — TENANT INFORMATION

_____ _____

UNIT #   ADDRESS   PHONE #

_____ _____

PRINCIPLE TENANT   CO-TENANT(S)

_____ _____ _____

EMERGENCY CONTACT   PHONE #   RELATIONSHIP

_____ _____ _____ _____

EMPLOYER   PHONE #   EXT.   SUPERVISOR

_____ _____ _____

DATE TENANCY BEGAN   RENT ($)   DATE RENT LAST RAISED

_____ _____

LAUNDRY DAYS / TIMES   PET(S)

_____ _____ _____

AUTO (MAKE, MODEL, COLOR)   LIC. PLATE #   PARKING SPACE #

LAST MONTH'S RENT: [   ] PAID ($ _____)

[   ] SEE CHART:

LAST MONTH'S RENT PAYMENTS		
DATE	PAYMENT	BALANCE
	$	$
	$	$
	$	$
	$	$
	$	$
	$	$
	$	$

(USE BACK IF NECESSARY)

51

B2.4 — TENANT LIST

Name(s)_____Rent $_____

Address _____Phone # _____

- -

Name(s)_____Rent $_____

Address _____Phone # _____

- -

Name(s)_____Rent $_____

Address _____Phone # _____

- -

Name(s)_____Rent $_____

Address _____Phone # _____

- -

Name(s)_____Rent $_____

Address _____Phone # _____

- -

Name(s)_____Rent $_____

Address _____Phone # _____

- -

Name(s)_____Rent $_____

Address _____Phone # _____

- -

Name(s)_____Rent $_____

Address _____Phone # _____

- -

Name(s)_____Rent $_____

Address _____Phone # _____

- -

B2.5 — SERVICE PROVIDER LIST

Trade	Name	Phone #
Plumber		
Electrician		
Carpenter		
Appliance repair		
Glass repair		
Painter		
Drywall repair		
General handyperson		
Yard maintenance		
Snow removal		
Carpet cleaner		
Tow truck		
Insurance agent		
Heating contractor		

B3.1 — PAINT INFORMATION

Unit #____ Address:_____ Date painted:_____

Name of painter:_____ Phone #:_____

_____

Paint type (Latex, Alkyd, etc.):_____ Sheen (Flat, Gloss, etc.)_____

Color name and #:_____ Tint base:_____

Brand, Manufacturer, Product #:_____

Where purchased:_____ Price: $ _____

Room(s) painted:_____

Surface(s) painted (walls, ceiling, trim, door, etc.):_____

Comments:_____

_____

Paint type (Latex, Alkyd, etc.):_____ Sheen (Flat, Gloss, etc.):_____

Color name and #:_____ Tint base:_____

Brand, Manufacturer, Product #:_____

Where purchased:_____ Price: $ _____

Room(s) painted:_____

Surface(s) painted (walls, ceiling, trim, door, etc.):_____

Comments:_____

B3.2 — MAINTENANCE LOG

Unit #_____   Address:_____

Work done:_____

_____

Date:_____   Cost: $ _____

Work done by:_____   Phone #:_____

Work done:_____

_____

Date:_____   Cost: $ _____

Work done by:_____   Phone #:_____

Work done:_____

_____

Date:_____   Cost: $ _____

Work done by:_____   Phone #:_____

Work done:_____

_____

Date:_____   Cost: $ _____

Work done by:_____   Phone #:_____

B3.3 — MAINTENANCE LOG

DATE	WORK DONE	TIME/COST

B3.4 — SPRING CHECKLIST

[   ]   Clean all snow-removal equipment and prepare it for storage (consult owners' manuals).

[   ]   **Store all winter equipment at back of storage facility, and bring all summer equipment to the front.**

[   ]   Have lawn mower serviced and blades sharpened.

[   ]   Check eavestroughs (clean if necessary).

[   ]   Re-evaluate drainage around foundation (re-grade if necessary).

[   ]   Clean, adjust, and lubricate door and window hardware where necessary.

[   ]   Clean window wells and windows.

[   ]   Check fire extinguishers, smoke detectors, and carbon monoxide detectors regularly.

[   ]   Install garden hose and check and repair leaks in hose or spigot.

[   ]   Re-seed bare spots on grass.

[   ]   Check for leaks around doors, windows, roof, and foundation walls, and repair where necessary.

[   ]   Clean and paint any exterior surface requiring refinishing.

[   ]   Repair or replace any damaged windows or screens.

[   ]   Clean debris from around the premises.

[   ]   Refasten or replace any loose or damaged siding or decking.

[   ]   Repair cracks in stucco, brick, and foundation walls.

[   ]   Shut down heating system when weather allows.

[   ]   Have air conditioning system cleaned and inspected (install portable units where used).

[   ]   Rake lawn to remove dead grass. Aerate the lawn.

[   ]   Apply a spring fertilizer to the lawn; add weed control as necessary.

[   ]   Prepare garden and plant flowers, etc.

[   ]   Prune trees and shrubs where necessary.

(add additional checklist items below)

[   ]   _____

[   ]   _____

[   ]   _____

[   ]   _____

[   ]   _____

[   ]   _____

[   ]   _____

[   ]   _____

[   ]   _____

B3.5 — SUMMER CHECKLIST

[   ] Re-evaluate drainage around foundation (re-grade if necessary).
[   ] Repair cracks in masonry walls, driveways, and walkways. Damp-proof masonry surfaces and seal asphalt surfaces.
[   ] Cut and water grass regularly (weed and fertilize if desired).
[   ] Weed and water gardens, trees, and shrubs regularly.
[   ] Clean under lawn mower (follow manufacturer's instructions).
[   ] Check roofing and flashing for damage, and repair or replace if necessary.
[   ] Pressure wash siding. Check for damage and repair or replace as necessary.
[   ] Maintain cooling and de-humidifier systems. Change filters frequently.
[   ] Inspect door and window weather-stripping and hardware. Oil, repair, or replace if necessary.
[   ] Check fire extinguishers, smoke detectors, and carbon monoxide detectors.
[   ] Check exposed water pipes for condensation. Insulate pipes if necessary.
[   ] Keep all exterior vents clear of obstructions.
[   ] Check for adequate attic ventilation. Excessive heat may indicate a problem exists, and may create problems in the future.
[   ] Check attic area for signs of moisture problems (wetness or water stains on insulation, roof trusses, and sheathing). Call a professional if any of these signs are present.
[   ] Clean and paint walls, window and door trims, and eavestroughs as necessary.
[   ] Clear debris from around the premises regularly.
[   ] Watch for signs of insect and rodent infestation.
[   ] Replace the washers in all faucets in every unit (It is better to do these all at the same time, once per year, than to do it each time a problem occurs).
[   ] Repair or replace window screens as necessary.

(add additional checklist items below)

[   ] _____
[   ] _____
[   ] _____
[   ] _____
[   ] _____
[   ] _____
[   ] _____
[   ] _____
[   ] _____

B3.6 — FALL CHECKLIST

[ ]   Re-seed any bare spots on the lawn.

[ ]   Apply a fall fertilizer to the lawn.

[ ]   Clean window wells and windows.

[ ]   Check window and door weather-stripping and hardware. Oil, repair, or replace as required.

[ ]   Caulk around windows and doors with a quality caulk.

[ ]   Check fire extinguishers, smoke detectors, and carbon monoxide detectors.

[ ]   Turn off the interior shut-off valve to the outdoor spigot, and fully open the outdoor spigot.

[ ]   Check the insulation in the attic (add more if necessary). Check for adequate ventilation.

[ ]   Cut back or remove plants in the garden.

[ ]   Cover small trees and shrubs with burlap and wooden A-frames.

[ ]   Clean eavestroughs and gutters.

[ ]   Have heating system cleaned and inspected. Replace filters monthly.

[ ]   Bleed the air from all radiators in a hot-water heating system.

[ ]   Duct tape all exposed duct joints in a forced-air heating system.

[ ]   Insulate all exposed water pipes in the basement, if you have not already done so.

[ ]   Wrap a heating cable around any water pipes in unheated areas and insulate.

[ ]   Seal up any holes or cracks on the exterior of the building that have not yet been sealed.

[ ]   Install heating cables on the lower courses of roof shingles (especially over doors) to prevent ice and snow build-up

[ ]   Clean all summer lawn and garden equipment.

[ ]   Store summer equipment at the back of the storage facility and bring winter equipment to the front.

[ ]   Replenish your supply of salt, sand, or kitty litter.

[ ]   Have snow-removal equipment serviced by a qualified professional.

(add additional checklist items below)

[ ]   _____

[ ]   _____

[ ]   _____

[ ]   _____

[ ]   _____

[ ]   _____

[ ]   _____

[ ]   _____

[ ]   _____

B3.7 — WINTER CHECKLIST

[ ] Ensure that chimney vents are cleared of snow at **all** times.

[ ] Maintain your supply of sand, salt, or kitty litter.

[ ] Keep eaves, gutters, and overhangs clear of all icicles.

[ ] Make a note of all problem icicle locations and areas on your roof without snow (re-assess the adequacy of insulation. If excessive melting occurs on the roof, call a professional).

[ ] Keep driveways and walkways clear of snow and ice.

[ ] Ensure all emergency exits are fully functional, and not snowed shut.

[ ] Remove snow from basement window wells, sills, etc.

[ ] Clear snow from all vents.

[ ] Clear snow from the area near the top of the foundation wall (where the siding begins).

[ ] Check fire extinguishers, smoke detectors, and carbon monoxide detectors regularly.

[ ] Remove excessive snow from roofs.

[ ] Check to see if any exterior windows are open (open windows may indicate that the heat is set too high). Lower heat level if this is the case, or adjust and/or repair heating ducts, radiator valves, etc.

[ ] Replace furnace filters monthly.

[ ] Maintain an adequate supply of water in humidifier(s).

[ ] Check radiators for airlocks and/or leaks.

[ ] Re-assess the adequacy of door and window weather-stripping.

[ ] Check that outdoor spigots (water valves) are open and shut off inside.

[ ] Keep outdoor meter and mail areas free from snow and ice.

[ ] Invest in a heating cable to wrap around water pipes. **Never thaw frozen pipes with a torch;** use a heating cable or a hair dryer instead or call a plumber.

[ ] Check for windows that ice-up or fog-up on the inside or between the panes. Repair or replace if necessary.

(add additional checklist items below)

[ ] _____

[ ] _____

[ ] _____

[ ] _____

[ ] _____

[ ] _____

[ ] _____

[ ] _____

[ ] _____

B3.8 — JOB ESTIMATE/QUOTE

(Circle above to indicate whether this is an estimate or a quote)

Customer name:_____ Phone #:_____

Job site:_____ Job description:_____

Prepared by:_____ Date:_____

Company name:_____ Phone #:_____

Start date:_____ Completion date:_____

Materials	Qty.	Unit Cost	Total Cost

Labor	Rate	Hours	Total Amount

Particulars:
_____
_____
_____
_____
_____

TOTAL COST: $_____   Signature_____

B4.1 — EQUIPMENT INVENTORY

The following information may prove to be invaluable in the event of theft, fire loss, or other loss. A more comprehensive inventory list may be obtained from your insurance agent. We recommend that whichever list you use, you give your insurance agent a copy and update it whenever you get new equipment. Save all receipts and provide copies of them to your insurance agent, if required.

- **Description:** Describe, in detail, the item as best as possible, identifying manufacturer name, color(s) and markings, and any distinctive markings.
- **Cost:** Record the actual price paid or approximate replacement value.
- **Model # and serial #:** Record model, and serial numbers (where applicable).

Description	Cost	Model#	Serial#

(use additional sheets if necessery)

B4.2 — UTILITIES AND APPLIANCE INVENTORY

This list is used to record information about utilities (furnace, boiler, water heater, etc.), and major appliances (refrigerators, stoves, dishwashers, disposers, etc.) so that you have a record of when they were bought, cost, model, and serial numbers.

ADDRESS: _____

Description	Date	Cost	Model#	Serial#

(use additional sheets if necessery)

63

B5.1 — FIRE SAFETY CHECKLIST

"Unless otherwise specified the owner is responsible for carrying out the provisions of this code." (Ontario Fire Code, Article 1.1.1.1.).

Below is a scaled down version of the standard owner (and agent for the owner) responsibilities regarding fire safety. Consult your local Fire Department for a complete list of these responsibilities and/or a copy of your local Fire Code. Never hesitate to ask questions of your local Fire Department — your questions may save lives.

Daily

[   ] Check all exit lights to ensure that they have not been damaged and that they are properly illuminated.

[   ] Check alarm panel to ensure that all indicator lights are functional and the appropriate lights are illuminated.

[   ] Check to ensure that all clutter (shoes, garbage, furniture, etc.) is removed from hallways, stairways, and other common spaces.

[   ] Keep all emergency exits clear of snow, ice, and clutter, and ensure proper operation of all emergency exit doors.

Monthly

[   ] Inspect all doors in fire separations (hall, stair, exit, apartment doors, etc.) for proper operation and closure.

[   ] Test all emergency lighting systems for proper operation.

[   ] Inspect all portable fire extinguishers for proper charge level and easy accessibility.

[   ] Test the fire alarm system for proper operation with system power on and using battery back-up (system power off). Ensure that all pull stations and smoke alarms will activate the alarm system when triggered. (Consult your system installer, monitoring company, or Fire Department for details.) **Always notify all tenants, system monitoring company, and Fire Department before each test.** (Tenant notification may be in the form of a notice posted in common areas indicating that fire alarm tests will take place at specified times each month.)

Annually

[   ] Conduct fire alarm drills in all buildings that have a fire alarm system. Even buildings that do not have a fire alarm system would benefit from a test. Encourage all tenants to practice an emergency evacuation plan (with a back-up plan).

[   ] Thoroughly inspect all fire extinguishers for proper operation. Replace the extinguishing agent in dry chemical extinguishers every 5-6 years or when needed.

[   ] Have qualified personnel conduct a complete test of the fire alarm system.

B5.2 — FIRE INSPECTION CHECKLIST

For the year_____

Fire alarm service provider:_____ Phone #:_____

Fire alarm monitoring company:_____

Emergency phone #:_____ Phone #:_____

Place your initials in the boxes below to indicate that these items were checked and in working order.

	J	F	M	A	M	J	J	A	S	O	N	D	Annual
Inspect doors													
Test emergency lighting													
Check fire extinguishers													
Test fire alarm with power on													
Test fire alarm with power off													
Check pull stations													
Check smoke detectors													

List the names of **all** persons who have initialled above:

Print name:_____ Initials:_____ Signature:_____

Print name:_____ Initials:_____ Signature:_____

Print name:_____ Initials:_____ Signature:_____

List **all** work performed on the fire alarm system this year (use back if necessary):_____

_____

_____

Annual inspection performed by: _____

Company name:_____ Phone #:_____

Results of annual inspection:_____

_____

_____

B5.3 — FIRE EMERGENCY PROCEDURES
(Management)
(See your local Fire Department for a complete list for your area and building type)

IF THE FIRE ALARM SOUNDS:

1. Contact the Fire Department immediately by telephoning **911** or _____.
   Give the name and address of the building and your name and telephone number.
2. Proceed to the main lobby and check the control panel to determine where the fire is located and to meet with the tenant who activated the fire alarm system.
3. Call all elevators to the main floor and remove them from service. If the building is equipped with fire fighters' elevators, prepare them for use.
4. The superintendent should have a list of all handicapped and infirm persons, complete with suite locations, in order to assist the Fire Department in locating those persons who may need help evacuating.
5. Upon arrival of the Fire Department, the superintendent must provide whatever assistance the Chief Fire Officer requires, including keys and information regarding the building and equipment.
6. The superintendent must be completely familiar with all the fire safety devices installed in the building, and must know where they are located and how they operate.
7. Alternate procedures must be in place to alert the building occupants if the fire alarm is out of service. Alternate safety procedures must also be in place, should any of the fire safety devices be removed from service for any reason.
8. The superintendent will be responsible for conducting regular maintenance duties on a daily, monthly, and yearly basis. (see forms B5.1 and B5.2, or contact your local Fire Department for more details).
9. Schematic diagrams showing the location of the building's fire emergency systems must be prepared and available for Fire Department use in an emergency.

List additional items pertaining to your building type and fire protection systems, and additional instructions from your local Fire Department:

_____
_____
_____
_____
_____
_____
_____
_____
_____
_____
_____
_____
_____